NATIVE AMERICAN NATIONS

THE CHEROKEE

BY BETTY MARCKS

CONSULTANT: TIM TOPPER,
CHEYENNE RIVER SIOUX

BLASTOFF! DISCOVERY

BELLWETHER MEDIA • MINNEAPOLIS, MN

Author's Statement of Positionality:
I am a white woman of European descent. As such, I can claim no direct lived experience of being a Native American. In writing this book, however, I have tried to be an ally by relying on sources by Native American writers and authors whenever possible and have worked to let their voices guide its content.

This edition first published in 2024 by Bellwether Media, Inc.

Library of Congress Cataloging-in-Publication Data

Names: Marcks, Betty, author.
Title: The Cherokee / by Betty Marcks.
Description: Minneapolis, MN : Bellwether Media, Inc., 2024. | Series: Blastoff! discovery: Native American nations | Includes bibliographical references and index. | Audience: Ages 7-13 | Audience: Grades 4-6 | Summary: "Engaging images accompany information about the Cherokee people. The combination of high-interest subject matter and narrative text is intended for students in grades 3 through 8" – Provided by publisher.
Identifiers: LCCN 2023025928 (print) | LCCN 2023025929 (ebook) | ISBN 9798886874419 (library binding) | ISBN 9798886876291 (ebook)
Subjects: LCSH: Cherokee Indians–Juvenile literature.
Classification: LCC E99.C5 M3395 2024 (print) | LCC E99.C5 (ebook) | DDC 305.897/557–dc23/eng/20230606
LC record available at https://lccn.loc.gov/2023025928
LC ebook record available at https://lccn.loc.gov/2023025929

Editor: Elizabeth Neuenfeldt Series Designer: Andrea Schneider
Book Designer: Laura Sowers

Printed in the United States of America, North Mankato, MN.

TABLE OF CONTENTS

THE PRINCIPAL PEOPLE 4

TRADITIONAL CHEROKEE LIFE 6

EUROPEAN CONTACT 12

LIFE TODAY 16

CONTINUING TRADITIONS 20

FIGHT TODAY, BRIGHT TOMORROW 24

TIMELINE 28

GLOSSARY 30

TO LEARN MORE 31

INDEX 32

THE PRINCIPAL PEOPLE

The Cherokees are a nation of Native American peoples. They believe their Creator gave them the name *Anigiduwagi*. It means "the principal people" or "the real people." The Cherokee homeland is in the Appalachian Mountains and surrounding areas of the southeastern United States. It includes parts of present-day Alabama, Georgia, Kentucky, North Carolina, South Carolina, Tennessee, and Virginia.

The **descendants** of **ancestral** Cherokees make up three tribes. They are the Cherokee Nation, the United Keetoowah Band of Cherokee Indians, and the Eastern Band of Cherokee Indians.

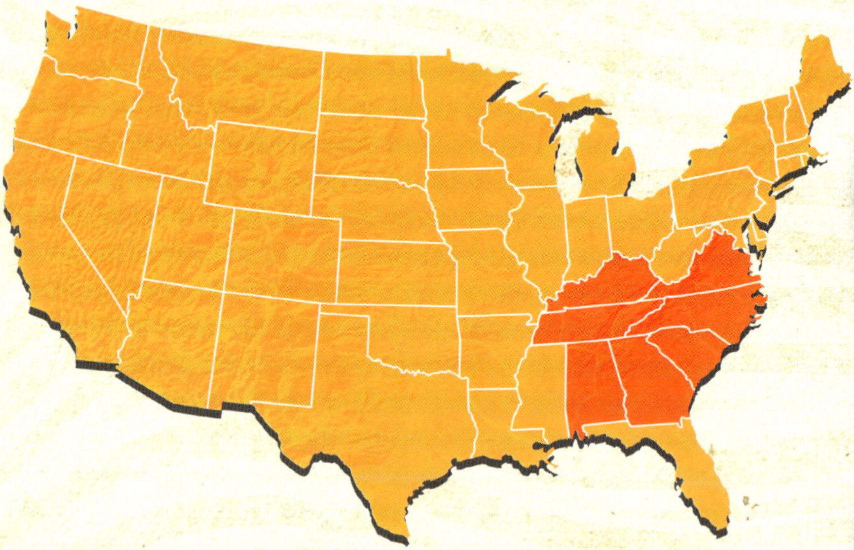

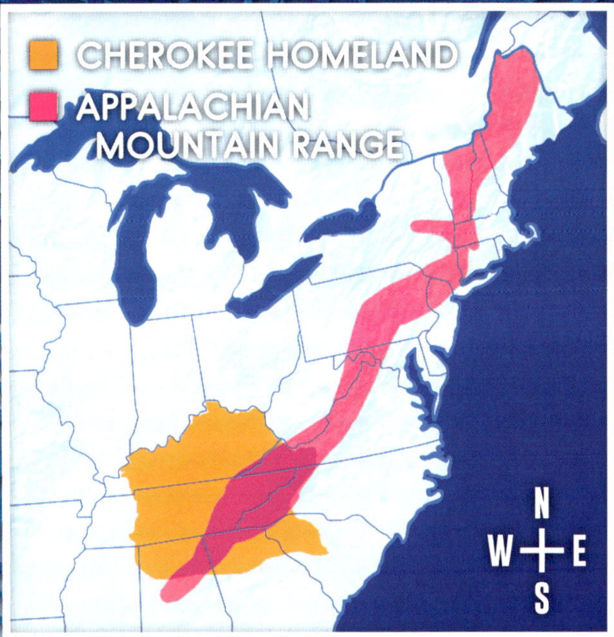
CHEROKEE HOMELAND
APPALACHIAN MOUNTAIN RANGE
N
W
E
S

APPALACHIAN MOUNTAINS

TRADITIONAL CHEROKEE LIFE

PAINT CLAN PILLAR

The Cherokees have a **clan** system. There are seven clans. Some clans are made up of smaller groups. Each clan is known for a skill or purpose that helps connect them to their **traditions** and **culture**. For example, members of the Paint Clan are known as healers.

PILLARS THAT REPRESENT THE SEVEN CHEROKEE CLANS AT THE CHOTA MEMORIAL IN TENNESSEE

SEVEN CHEROKEE CLANS

The seven Cherokee clans are Wolf, Blue, Long Hair, Paint, Bird, Deer, and Wild Potato.

Each clan is **matrilineal**. People are born into their mother's family and clan. Ancestral Cherokee women were the heads of their families. They owned their homes. Women and men were equal members of their communities.

Ancestral Cherokees lived in small communities. Villages had a Peace Chief and a War Chief. They were also led by a village **council**. But everyone in a community could share their thoughts.

ILLUSTRATION OF A CHEROKEE VILLAGE

RECREATION OF A CHEROKEE LOG HOUSE

LOG HOUSES

Many Cherokees began living in homes made from logs in the 1800s.

Villages were often located near rivers or streams. Some were surrounded by a large wooden fence. The Cherokees lived in wattle and daub homes. They were made of wooden poles covered with vines, young trees, and mud. Village council meetings and **ceremonies** took place in council houses. These buildings were often seven-sided. Each side represented one of the seven clans.

CHEROKEE RESOURCES

Ancestral Cherokees were farmers, gatherers, and hunters. Women mostly grew corn, beans, and squash. They also gathered roots, fruits, and nuts. Men used bows and arrows to hunt deer and bears. Blowguns were used to take down smaller animals such as rabbits, birds, and squirrels.

Ancestral Cherokees were skilled craftspeople. They wove baskets from river cane and oak. Each clan had their own basket pattern. They were also known for their pottery. They made jugs, bowls, and other dishes from clay.

WOVEN BASKETS

ILLUSTRATION OF A CHEROKEE CRAFTSPERSON

EUROPEAN CONTACT

In 1540, the Cherokees met Europeans for the first time. The Spanish explorer Hernando de Soto and his men entered Cherokee land. The Cherokees suffered from Spanish attacks and illnesses. But they fought back. In the 1600s, they began trading with Europeans for goods.

ILLUSTRATION OF SIR ALEXANDER CUMING, A SCOTTISH ADVENTURER, VISITING CHEROKEES AROUND 1730

Colonists pressured the Cherokees for land throughout the 1700s. The Cherokees sided with the British in trading and wars. They hoped this would help them keep their land. But fighting between colonists and the Cherokees increased in the late 1700s. The Cherokees were forced to give up more and more land.

Some Cherokees **adapted** to an American lifestyle in the 1800s. They formed a government like that of the U.S. But **settlers** moved onto Cherokee land. A **treaty** signed in 1835 ordered all Cherokees to move to what is now Oklahoma. Thousands of Cherokee people were forced to march the **Trail of Tears** in 1838.

Those who survived the march eventually received land in Oklahoma. Their descendants make up the Cherokee Nation and the United Keetoowah Band of Cherokee Indians. A small group of Cherokees hid in the mountains to escape the march. Their descendants became the Eastern Band of Cherokee Indians.

ᏣᎳᎩ ᏧᎴᎯᏌᏅᎯ

CHEROKEE PHOENIX.

NEW ECHOTA, THURSDAY FEBRUARY 21, 1828.

A WRITTEN LANGUAGE

A man named Sequoyah created a writing system for the Cherokee language in 1821. The writing system was used in the *Cherokee Phoenix* newspaper in 1828. It is the oldest and longest running Native American newspaper. Today, it is available online.

FAMOUS CHEROKEE

MARY GOLDA ROSS

BIRTHDAY August 9, 1908

DEATH April 29, 2008

FAMOUS FOR

The first Native American female aerospace engineer who helped put people into space

LIFE TODAY

Today, the Cherokees are a nation of more than 450,000 people. Some members live on their **reservation**. Others live throughout the U.S. and the world. Most Cherokees are active in American culture. But they also honor their **heritage**.

The Cherokee Nation is the largest of the three tribes. It has 14 counties in Oklahoma. The United Keetoowah Band of Cherokee Indians is located in Tahlequah, Oklahoma. The Eastern Band of Cherokee Indians is in North Carolina. The city of Cherokee is its capital.

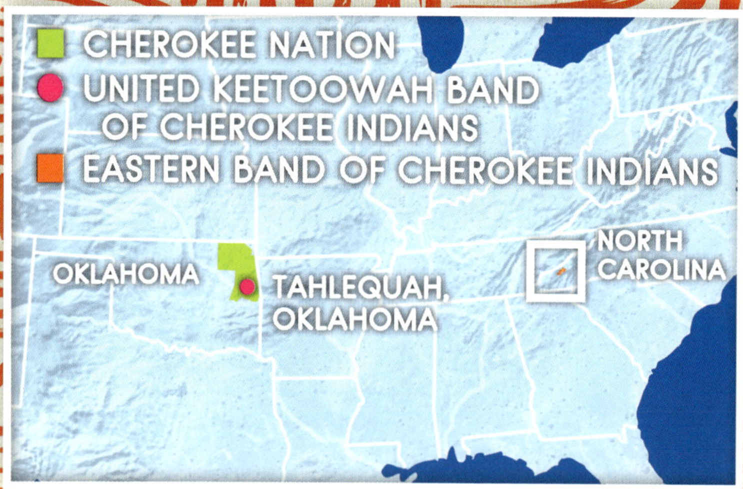

CHEROKEE, NORTH CAROLINA, CAPITAL OF THE EASTERN BAND OF CHEROKEE INDIANS

Each Cherokee tribe is an independent nation. The Principal Chief leads the Cherokee Nation's government. A 17-member Tribal Council creates laws. The Nation has a Supreme Court and district courts. The Eastern Band's government is organized similarly to the Cherokee Nation's government. Its Tribal Council has 12 members. The United Keetoowah Band's government is led by the Chief and Tribal Council.

Each government owns many businesses. Each year, thousands of people visit the casinos each nation owns. **Tourism** allows each nation to teach the public Cherokee history and culture.

GOVERNMENT OF THE CHEROKEE NATION

EXECUTIVE

- Principal Chief
- Deputy Principal Chief
- 7-member cabinet

LEGISLATIVE

- 17-member Tribal Council

JUDICIAL

- Supreme Court
- district courts

HARRAH'S CHEROKEE CASINO RESORT IN CHEROKEE, NORTH CAROLINA

MEDICAL SCHOOL

The Cherokee Nation and Oklahoma State University opened a medical school in 2021. It is in the Nation's capital, Tahlequah, Oklahoma.

CONTINUING TRADITIONS

WILD RAMPS

Celebrations are one of the ways the Cherokees honor their traditions. The Rainbows and Ramps Festival is held each March in Cherokee, North Carolina. Ramps are wild onions that the Cherokees have used for thousands of years. The Cherokee Voices Festival happens each June. People dance, practice storytelling, and more.

The Cherokee National Holiday occurs every September. It honors the signing of the Cherokee **Constitution**. It also celebrates Cherokee heritage and families coming together. People play traditional sports such as stickball and marbles. They make traditional arts. People watch a parade and listen to the Cherokee National Youth Choir.

CHEROKEE NATIONAL HOLIDAY PARADE

STICKBALL

Games have been important to the Cherokees for thousands of years. Stickball was once played to settle disagreements and avoid war. Now it is a social game. Players use two sticks with pockets to catch a small ball. The rules of stickball can change from game to game.

Cherokee artists use traditional practices to make modern art. Jane Osti is a potter who makes paddle stamp pots. She adds her personal style to the methods of her ancestors. Basket weaving is another important tradition. Vivian Cottrell is a weaver who teaches the double-weave style. Ancestral Cherokees used this weave to make baskets from river cane.

CHEROKEE STAMP POTS

The Cherokees began using textured paddles to make stamp pots more than 2,000 years ago. The texture on stamp pots makes them easier to hold onto, holds heat better than a smooth texture, and adds beauty!

JANE OSTI MAKING A STAMP POT

STAMP POT

STAMP PADDLES

FIGHT TODAY, BRIGHT TOMORROW

The Cherokees are fighting to make their voices heard. The 1835 treaty promised the Cherokees a seat in the U.S. **Congress**. The Cherokee Nation chose Kimberly Teehee in 2019 to be the first representative. Many Congress members support the decision. But as of early 2023, Congress has failed to seat her.

A seat for the Cherokee Nation in Congress would show that the U.S. government is taking steps to right many of its past wrongs. It would allow the Cherokee Nation to introduce and support laws that affect Native Americans.

KIMBERLY TEEHEE WITH U.S. PRESIDENT BARACK OBAMA IN 2012

KIMBERLY TEEHEE
SPEAKING IN 2019

PRINCIPAL CHIEF OF THE CHEROKEE NATION, CHUCK HOSKIN, JR.

The Cherokees have faced many hardships throughout their history. But they work to keep their culture and traditions alive. The Cherokee Nation hosts classes that focus on history and culture. Some are being developed that focus on certain events such as the Trail of Tears.

The Cherokee Nation's Principal Chief believes the classes will help the Nation continue to be successful. Students are encouraged to share what they learn with family and friends. The Cherokees hope people feel more connected to their heritage!

THE CHEROKEE LANGUAGE

The Cherokee language is in danger of being lost. Benjamin Frey helped create a smartphone operating system that uses the written form of Cherokee. There are also online programs that help people learn the language.

STUDENTS LEARNING CHEROKEE

TIMELINE

1540

Spanish explorer Hernando de Soto is the first European to enter Cherokee land

1600s

The Cherokees and Europeans begin trading goods

1785

The Treaty of Hopewell is signed, determining the boundaries of Cherokee land

1821

Sequoyah creates a Cherokee writing system

1827

The first Cherokee constitution is passed

1866

The Treaty of 1866 is signed, promising no one will try to settle on Cherokee land

1985

Wilma Mankiller becomes the first female Principal Chief of the Cherokee Nation

1838

Thousands of Cherokees are forced to march from their homeland to Oklahoma on the Trail of Tears

1942

Mary Golda Ross becomes the first Native American female aerospace engineer

2019

Kimberly Teehee is chosen as the first person to represent the Cherokee Nation in the U.S. House of Representatives

GLOSSARY

adapted—changed over a period of time

ancestral—related to relatives who lived long ago

ceremonies—sets of actions performed in a particular way, often as part of religious worship

clan—a group of people who share a common ancestor

colonists—people sent by a government to a new region or territory

Congress—the group of people who make laws for the United States

constitution—the basic laws and principles of a nation

council—a group of people who meet to run a government

culture—the beliefs, arts, and ways of life in a place or society

descendants—people related to a person or group of people who lived at an earlier time

heritage—the traditions, achievements, and beliefs that are part of the history of a group of people

matrilineal—related to or based on following a family line through the mother

reservation—land set aside by the U.S. government for the forced removal of a Native American community from their original land

settlers—people who move to live in a new region

tourism—the business of people traveling to visit other places

traditions—customs, ideas, or beliefs handed down from one generation to the next

Trail of Tears—the forced relocation of up to 100,000 Native Americans from their homelands to areas farther west in the 1830s

treaty—an official agreement between two groups

TO LEARN MORE

AT THE LIBRARY

Bird, F. A. *Cherokee.* Minneapolis, Minn.: Abdo Publishing, 2022.

Rogers, Andrea L. *Mary and the Trail of Tears: A Cherokee Removal Survival Story.* North Mankato, Minn.: Capstone, 2020.

Sorell, Traci. *Classified: The Secret Career of Mary Golda Ross, Cherokee Aerospace Engineer.* Minneapolis, Minn.: Millbrook Press, 2021.

ON THE WEB

FACTSURFER

Factsurfer.com gives you a safe, fun way to find more information.

1. Go to www.factsurfer.com.
2. Enter "the Cherokee" into the search box and click 🔍.
3. Select your book cover to see a list of related content.

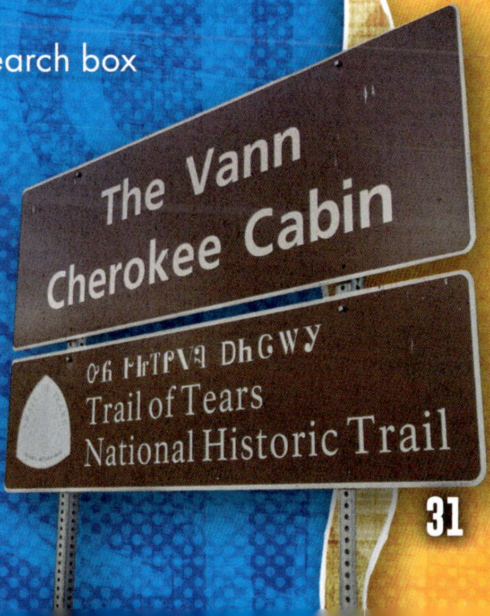

INDEX

Appalachian Mountains, 4, 5, 14
arts, 21, 23
Cherokee, North Carolina, 16, 17, 19, 20
Cherokee Nation, 4, 14, 16, 18, 19, 24, 26, 27
Cherokee National Holiday, 21
Cherokee National Youth Choir, 21
Cherokee resources, 10
Cherokee stamp pots, 23
Cherokee Voices Festival, 20
chiefs, 8, 18, 26, 27
clans, 6, 7, 9, 11
Cottrell, Vivian, 23
council, 8, 9, 18
culture, 6, 11, 16, 18, 26
Eastern Band of Cherokee Indians, 4, 14, 16, 17, 18
Frey, Benjamin, 27
future, 24, 26, 27
government of the Cherokee Nation, 18
heritage, 16, 21, 27
history, 4, 7, 8, 9, 10, 11, 12, 13, 14, 15, 18, 19, 21, 22, 23, 24, 25, 26
homeland, 4, 5, 12, 13, 14
homes, 7, 9
language, 15, 27
map, 4, 5, 16
members, 16
name, 4
Osti, Jane, 23
Rainbows and Ramps Festival, 20
religion, 4
reservation, 16
Ross, Mary Golda, 15
Sequoyah, 15
Soto, Hernando de, 12
stickball, 21, 22
Tahlequah, Oklahoma, 16, 19
Teehee, Kimberly, 24, 25
timeline, 28–29
tourism, 18
traditions, 6, 8, 9, 10, 11, 20, 21, 22, 23, 26
Trail of Tears, 14, 26
treaty, 14, 24
United Keetoowah Band of Cherokee Indians, 4, 14, 16, 18
U.S. government, 14, 24

The images in this book are reproduced through the courtesy of: George Rose/ Contributor/ Getty Images, front cover; Bob Pardue - Signs/ Alamy, p. 3; EWY Media, pp. 4-5; Brian Stansberry/ Wikipedia, p. 6; Nativestock.com/ Marilyn Angel Wynn/ Alamy, pp. 6-7, 11 (woven baskets); ibusca, p. 8; marak kasula/ Alamy, p. 9; Shane Adams, p. 10 (river cane); Luc Novovitch/ Alamy, p. 10 (blowgun, darts); h.jack, p. 10 (thistle); TippyTortue, p. 10 (white oak tree); piemags/ DCM/ Alamy, p. 11; John Sartain/ Wikipedia, p. 12; The Print Collector/ Alamy, pp. 12-13; BD Images/ Alamy, p. 14; Elias Boudinot and Isaac H. Harris/ Wikipedia, p. 15 (a written language); NASA/ Courtesy of the National Museum of the American Indian, p. 15 (Mary Golda Ross); Jacob Boomsma, pp. 16-17; unknown/ Wikipedia, p. 18; Ian Dagnall/ Alamy, p. 19 (Harrah's Cherokee Casino); OSUCHS marketing/ Wikipedia, p. 20; James Aloysius Mahan V, p. 20; Susan Vineyard/ Alamy, p. 21; NB/ TRAN/ Alamy, p. 22; U.S. National Archives and Records Administration/ Wikipedia, p. 23 (Jane Osti, stamp paddles); Reading Room 2020/ Alamy, p. 23 (stamp pot); Pete Souza/ Wikipedia, p. 24; Sue Ogrocki/ AP Images, pp. 24-25, 27; Michael Woods/ AP Images, p. 26; John Sartain/ Wikipedia, p. 28 (1540); Library of Congress/ Wikipedia, p. 28 (1821); Charles Bird King/ Wikipedia, p. 28 (1827); Allen Creative/ Steve Allen/ Alamy, p. 29 (1838); Phebe Hemphill, Benjamin Sowards/ Wikipedia, p. 29 (1985); Lonnie Tague for the Justice Department/ Wikipedia, p. 29 (2019).